THE BELIEVER'S POSSESSION

God has endowed the church: the body of believers of which Jesus Christ is the head, with so much that can't be exhausted. That is the loving display of the benevolent nature of our God. I once heard a preacher say that God is more willing to give than we are willing to receive. This is a conclusive truth. However, I said this to draw your attention to the light of God's gifts to as many who have already received Christ.

These endowments are potent and eternal. They came into the believer's spirit as a result of Christ's death, burial and resurrection. The Christian, as a result of this, comes into a full and complete union with deity. This opportunity now presents a different kind of being which is tied with omnipotence.

However, one thing seems to amaze me. It is the fact that most of the disciples that were with Jesus during his earthly sojourn, could rarely tell what actually happened in the spiritual when Christ died, was buried and resurrected and what we have become as a result. We don't group the reality of the substitutionary sacrifice and the inherent blessings that have been bestowed on us Christians.

> ***3For I delivered unto you first of all that which I also received, how that***
> ***Christ died for our sins according to the scriptures; 4And that he was***
> ***buried, and that he rose again the third day according to the scriptures:***
> ***5And that he was seen of Cephas, then of the twelve: 6After that, he was***
> ***seen of above five hundred brethren at once; of whom the greater part***
> ***remain unto this present, but some are fallen asleep. 7After that, he was***
> ***seen of James; then of all the apostles. 8And last of all he was seen of me***
> ***also, as of one born out of due time. 9For I am the least of the apostles,***
> ***that am not meet to be called an apostle, because I persecuted the church***
> ***of God. 10But by the grace of God I am what I am: and his grace which was***
> ***bestowed upon me was not in vain; but I laboured more abundantly than***
> ***they all: yet not I, but the grace of God which was with me.***
> **1 Corinthians 15:3-10;**

After Christ had resurrected and appeared unto above five hundred brethren and even the apostles, Paul was yet not in Christ. He was a staunch persecutor of the body of Christ. He describes himself in 1 cor. 15:8-9, as one born out of due time (not having had the opportunity to see Jesus Physically) and as the least of all the apostles because the apostles could tell what Jesus looked like physically.

[4]And he fell to the earth, and heard a voice saying unto him, Saul, Saul, why persecutest thou me? [17]And Ananias went his way, and entered into the house; and putting his hands on him said, Brother Saul, the Lord, even Jesus, that appeared unto thee in the way as thou camest, hath sent me, that thou mightest receive thy sight, and be filled with the Holy Ghost. **Acts 9:4,17;**

[14]And he said, The God of our fathers hath chosen thee, that thou shouldest know his will, and see that Just One, and shouldest hear the voice of his mouth. [18]And saw him saying unto me, Make haste, and get thee quickly out of Jerusalem: for they will not receive thy testimony concerning me. **Acts 22:14,18;**

*[1]Am I am not an apostle? am I not free? have I not seen Jesus Christ our Lord? are not ye my work in the Lord?***1 Corinthians 9:1,**

After Paul met with Jesus, he functioned by the grace of God bestowed on him and labored more abundantly than the apostles.

Reading through one of Paul's epistles, especially to the Christians in Rome, I was startled at Paul's statement when he declared, *"In the day when God shall judge the secrets of men by Jesus Christ* ***according to my Gospel****"*. And in Romans16:15-26, he declares again, **"according to my Gospel"**. I thought within myself, "How could one speak in such an impudent manner in God's word?" On a second thought, I felt if God would allow such a statement in his word then this was undoubtedly the mind of the Spirit. And later i thought again, "according to my gospel?" What gospel could he possibly be talking about? Then I saw the book of Galatians 1:6-12, and Eph. 3:1-12;

[11]But I certify you, brethren, that the gospel which was preached of me is not after man. [12]For I neither received it of man, neither was I taught it, but by the revelation of Jesus Christ. **Galatians 1:11-12.**

From the light of these scriptures I saw for myself how that Paul declares that this gospel of his was not received of man, neither was he taught. It was a gospel given to him by revelation. It was the gospel of Jesus Christ given to him directly from God the Father.

This classic gospel is the one he summarized in **1 Corinthians 15:3-4**

[3]For I delivered unto you first of all that which I also received, how that Christ died for our sins according to the scriptures; [4]And that he was buried, and that he rose again the third day according to the scriptures:

This was the focus of Paul's gospel. He preached the complete news of Christ as our substitutionary sacrifice. In order words, that Christ became us in God's redemptive plan and as a result, we have become all that he is in the eyes of Justice.

However, the whole detail of God's redemptive plan is contained in these main parts of redemption.

The first part of the redemptive plan I would like us to consider is the legal aspect of the redemptive plan of God. This reveals to us what God did for us in Christ Jesus. If you would observe, you'll simply discover that the predicate used in my last statement is in the past tense verb – did. This means that the legal side of God's redemptive plan in his word is always indicated to be something that had already been done as a result of Christ death, burial and resurrection. The legal side of our redemption is simply a pointer to what legally belongs to us now as new creations. Let's look at a vivid example.

***[13]Who hath delivered us from the power of darkness, and hath translated us into the kingdom of his dear Son*: Colossians 1:13.**

From this scripture, you can see the verb "hath delivered", used to depict a reference to the legal side of our redemption. So this is one of such episodes in which what God did for us in Christ is clearly presented to us. By this, as a result, we have our deliverance as new creations in Christ.

Furthermore, the vital side of our redemption is what the Holy Spirit is doing in the new creation now through the word of God. This is a present work of God in us by the Spirit. I would like us to take a look at this.

***[13]For it is God which worketh in you both to will and to do of his good pleasure.* Philippians 2:13**

From this scripture, you can see that for the born again child of God, the father i s at work in him, causing the believer to go after the will of God and to do his good pleasures always.

Considering the legal and vital sides of our redemption decisively will bring us to a point where we are able to see what we have in Christ as believers in the kingdom of God.

CHAPTER ONE
REDEMPTION

Adam, the first man that God created, was created with the father's nature in him. He was created in and functioned in God's class. He was God's representative on the earth. He had the life of God, the mind of God and the abilities of God in him till his fall.

When Adam fell, he died spiritually and consequently became a carrier of the nature of Satan. Before this time, God conferred upon him the authority to dominate or rule the entire universe. Surprisingly, he turned this legally conferred dominion over into the hands of God's enemy. This act was a treasonable felony as God considers it. This high treason was what threw the Spirit of man to become united with a death-doomed nature. As a result of this, man legally came under the dominion of Satan.

The nature of Satan in the Spirit of man was however, the sole reason for redemption. The purpose of redemption was to deliver us from Satan's dominion so that we could now receive the nature of God with which we would serve the living God.

This is one beautiful experience that Christ was sent to introduce to us when he died and was buried then it was consummated when he was made alive in the Spirit and resurrected.

> ***11But Christ being come an high priest of good things to come, by a greater and more perfect tabernacle, not made with hands, that is to say, not of this building; 12Neither by the blood of goats and calves, but by his own blood he entered in once into the holy place, having obtained eternal redemption for us.*** **Hebrews 9:11-12**

It was the responsibility of high priests in the Old Testament to offer sacrifice to God and for the people. And this was to have a resultant effect. It could either be forgiveness of sins, for atonement, for deliverance or for answers to prayers. But Jesus, as the bible describes, was the high priest that would introduce good things by his own sacrifice. The sacrifice however was not an animal but himself. Therefore, he secured eternal redemption for us with his blood.

The implication is automatic. If Christ Jesus, obtained eternal redemption for us, then we are eternally delivered and Satan, eternally defeated. So I can now shout, "Hallelujah! Satan is forever defeated". I am completely free. There is no more room for condemnation in my life. Satan cannot bring me under guilt anymore. I am more than a conqueror. I am a victor in Christ. Let's pause a while and take a look at verse 15.

> ***[15]And for this cause he is the mediator of the new testament, that by means of death, for the redemption of the transgressions that were under the first testament, they which are called might receive the promise of eternal inheritance.*** **Hebrews 9:15.**

Jesus came in between the two testaments so that by his death which brought our redemption, the new creation in Christ will have the reign of all the curses encapsulated in the first testament, brought to an end. And as if all these were not enough, they would now become legal and eternal owners of what God has given them in Christ Jesus by right. Isn't this beautiful, to know that we are not under any curse again by the reason of or redemption?

> ***[13]Christ hath redeemed us from the curse of the law, being made a curse for us: for it is written, Cursed is every one that hangeth on a tree: [14]That the blessing of Abraham might come on the Gentiles through Jesus Christ; that we might receive the promise of the Spirit through faith. [15]Brethren, I speak after the manner of men; Though it be but a man's covenant, yet if it be confirmed, no man disannulleth, or addeth thereto. [16]Now to Abraham and his seed were the promises made. He saith not, And to seeds, as of many; but as of one, And to thy seed, which is Christ*** **.Galatians 3:13 – 16**

Yes! Christ became a curse for us. This has left us eternally blessed and eternal blessings. Oh, I wish you would boldly declare: I am blessed. I am an eternal blessing. I am a blessing to those around me. The blessings of Abraham are in my life. I am born again. I am born a blessing. I have the seed of greatness in me.

[3]Blessed be the God and Father of our Lord Jesus Christ, who hath blessed us with all spiritual blessings in heavenly places in Christ: **Ephesians 1:3.**

This is one reason why our life has got to be radiant. God has blessed you. The more you declare this, the more the blessings are stirred up inside you. The more God will direct people to favour you. If only you could choose to remove the I am in need theory from you mentality. Then you'll find yourself talking like God because God can never be in need. I am eternally blessed. It is a present day reality.

[26]For then must he often have suffered since the foundation of the world: but now once in the end of the world hath he appeared to put away sin by the sacrifice of himself. **Hebrews 9:26**

This is what those who have not come to Christ are missing. It is the benefit of being completely free from the authority of Satan. But to the Christian, it is a joyous reality: the joyous reality that we can now fellowship with God. We are no longer captives of Satan. We are in right standing with God because his nature indwells us. His life is our inheritance.
When we were Satan's subjects, we were simply sense-ruled. But now, thanks be to God, we are no longer under his authority.

[12]Giving thanks unto the Father, which hath made us meet to be partakers of the inheritance of the saints in light: [13]Who hath delivered us from the power of darkness, and hath translated us into the kingdom of his dear Son: [14]In whom we have redemption through his blood, even the forgiveness of sins: **Colossians 1:12 – 14**

This reality was so evident and Satan has never forgotten that encounter. He was conquered forever. He suffered this perpetual defeat that would leave him eternally regretting.

[8]Which none of the princes of this world knew: for had they known it, they would not have crucified the Lord of glory. **1 Corinthians 2:8**

Satan did not know that God's plan was for Jesus to die in our place. So the implication was now the fact that Jesus' victory was our victory. All that he did on the cross was entirely for us. Before Jesus was crucified, it was so evident that we needed his redemption. This was why Jesus, our perfect redeemer came so as to make us perfectly redeemed. Therefore if Jesus conquered the entire hoardes of hell, in the eyes of justice, we were the ones that conquered them.

> [14]***Forasmuch then as the children are partakers of flesh and blood, he also himself likewise took part of the same; that through death he might destroy him that had the power of death, that is, the devil; [15]And deliver them who through fear of death were all their lifetime subject to bondage.*** **Hebrews 2:14-15**

Jesus, the word of God became flesh. The living logos of God came in the form of a human so that by his death he might end the reign of the one who had the power of death – the devil. Before Jesus' death, Satan was the God of this world. Now don't forget that it was the authority God gave to Adam that he transferred to Satan when he submitted to him. Satan also had the power of death. He would transmit spiritual death and this will consequently produce physical death. This was the reason why when God permitted him to try Job, he said but don't touch his soul. This was because Satan had the power to touch the soul of Job. But after the death of Christ on the cross, Satan ceased to be the god of this world. He also lost that power of death. The new creations in Christ are now the gods of this world. We have conquered Satan. Jesus conquered him on our behalf.

> [8]***...For this purpose the Son of God was manifested, that he might destroy the works of the devil.*** **1 John 3:8**

The principal purpose of the crucifixion of Christ was so that the effects of Satan's works would be completely destroyed. So the new creation can now say, thanks be to God, Satan's works are shattered from my life. Let's see another interesting part of this adventurous display.

> [15]***And having spoiled principalities and powers, he made a shew of them openly, triumphing over them in it.*** **Colossians 2:15**

Oh! I just love this scripture. You know that Jesus died on the cross but the spiritual reality is that he was made sin with sins of whole world. So God saw him as we were. He became us – sinners because our sins were laid on his Spirit. And of course you know that, anyone who dies in sin must of necessity go to hell. So

Jesus, in order to fulfill the demands of justice, had to qualify for hell because he had our sinful nature upon his spirit. 2 Corinthians 5:21 says, "He was made sin, who knew no sin, that we might become the righteousness of God in Christ." Since he was made sin, he had to go to hell. Now in Colossians 2:15, there is a pointer. Anyone who goes to hell will be captured by principalities and power, and would subsequently be required to bow to the Lordship of Satan. Jesus was therefore captured in hell by the principalities and powers of darkness. But when he was required to bow to Satan's Lordship, Jesus refused to bow. That was when he disarmed Satan of his authority, took the keys of death and of hell from him and walked out triumphantly from hell. This was the reason he qualified to be made alive in the Spirit and then resurrected from the dead. Hallelujah.

> [18]***I am he that liveth, and was dead; and, behold, I am alive for evermore, Amen; and have the keys of hell and of death.*** **Revelation 1:18**

This was an absolute perfection of our redemption. Now we are free to relate and associate with divinity. Now we have come into a vital union with God. We can live by the Spirit and not by our senses. We can now function by revelation and not by sense knowledge. We can walk in the Spirit and not fulfill the cravings of the flesh. We can now worship the father in Spirit and truth. We have become heirs of God and joint heirs with Christ. We are now born again not of corruptible seed. We can now rejoice in our bold declaration of the truth that now we are sons of God.

> [2]***Beloved, now are we the sons of God, and it doth not yet appear what we shall be: but we know that, when he shall appear, we shall be like him; for we shall see him as he is.*** **1 John 3:2**

We are the redeemed of the Lord. We have our complete deliverance from the enemy and all other limitations. We have eternal redemption.

> [7]***In whom we have redemption through his blood, the forgiveness of sins, according to the riches of his grace;*** **Ephesians 1:7**

CHAPTER TWO
ETERNAL LIFE

The whole essence of Christ's coming can be seen in John 10:10; ...but I came that they might have life and have it to the full. He was talking to the Pharisees at this time. But wait a minute. If he were talking to the Pharisees he couldn't have been talking to the physically dead ones when he said I came that you might have life. They were physically alive yet Jesus said he came so they might have life.

What life could he possibly be talking about then? It couldn't have been a physical life, since the people he was taking to were physically alive. He was talking about a super life. It is a higher kind of life. It is the God kind of life. He was talking about eternal life. This was the reason why he came. And he came to give it to the full. At this point, i'd really like to show you something you would definitely like to see.

> ***8But what saith it? The word is nigh thee, even in thy mouth, and in thy heart: that is, the word of faith, which we preach; 9That if thou shalt confess with thy mouth the Lord Jesus, and shalt believe in thine heart that God hath raised him from the dead, thou shalt be saved. 10For with the heart man believeth unto righteousness; and with the mouth confession is made unto salvation.*** **Romans 10:8-10**

There is an amazing truth in this scripture about the one who wants to be a Christian. It is the fact that he is not even required to confess his sins in order to be born again. In verse 9, we see that all the sinner needs to confess is, "the Lord Jesus". One day I had to ask myself two important questionson this subject. Firstly, "Why would God not want us to confess our sins in order to be born again". And secondly, "why is the requirement simply confessing Jesus as Lord?" After giving it some deep thoughts, and comparing scripture with scripture, I discovered that if confession of sins were a requirement, then God will require you to confess all of your sins (this includes the ones you committed in your childhood days) before salvation would be granted. Even if you tried, you couldn't remember all of them and so you couldn't have qualified to be born again. So thank God it wasn't the requirement. Secondly, another reason why i thought God wouldn't require a confession of your sins as a prerequisite for salvation was because there is no life in your sins. I would like to add another point to these two. Imagine someone who always confesses lack, he's simply amplifying its possibilities and as such, that negative propensity will be empowered to happen. So also if the same person starts confessing divine prosperity he'll have succeeded in creating the right atmosphere of favour or prosperity. So imagine one who confesses sins. He can't possibly have the power to live above it. Then the second questions answer now becomes clearer. There is life in the name of Jesus. So when we confess his name, that divine life is imparted to our spirit. This life is eternal life.

Eternal life, against the theology of some preachers is not the life that will be given to us when Jesus comes back again. The kind of life they are simply talking about is an immortal body. But the eternal life is in the Spirit and not the body (even though it regularly transmits life to the body as we function in the Spirit). Eternal life is God's kind of life. All animals have the animal kind of life and he same goes for all plants. Humans have the human life but born again Christian have eternal life or the God kind of life.

> ***11And this is the record, that God hath given to us eternal life, and this life is in his Son. 12He that hath the Son hath life; and he that hath not the Son of God hath not life. 13These things have I written unto you that believe on the name of the Son of God; that ye may know that ye have eternal life, and that ye may believe on the name of the Son of God.*** **1 John 5:11 – 13**

Did you observe those tenses? Verse 11 says that God has (already) given to us eternal life. John was talking to Christians (1 John 1:1-3). He said this to bring to their knowledge that God had given them his kind of life.

In this world, there are two basic kinds of life - the ordinary and the extraordinary. The ordinary kind of life is the normal, natural life that every other person lives on the earth. But the other kind of life is a higher, supernatural and divine life. In the Greek, the ordinary, normal life is called "Tsuke" but the super life is called "Zoe". Zoe is the substance of God's being. In it is God's divine ability. With that life, we become the evidence of the potency of heaven. Accordingly to verse 12, he that has the son has life (Zoe) but he that has not the son hath not life (Tsuke)s. Then verse 13 is just so beautiful: ...that ye may know that ye have eternal life. With this life in the spirit of the Christian, nothing can be impossible to him or her. With this life, no weapon formed against you can prosper. With this life, you cast out demons, heal the sick, and do many mighty works. It is divinity dominating and gaining the ascendancy over humanity.

> [17]*And these signs shall follow them that believe; In my name shall they cast out devils; they shall speak with new tongues;* [18]*They shall take up serpents; and if they drink any deadly thing, it shall not hurt them; they shall lay hands on the sick, and they shall recover.* **Mark 16:17-18;**
>
> [19]***Behold, I give unto you power to tread on serpents and scorpions, and over all the power of the enemy: and nothing shall by any means hurt you.*** **Luke 10:19**

With this life, we can do things beyond human comprehension. Our lives become driven by the ability of God. We become living wonders as a result of his life. We become transmitters of the conquering life of the Father. We become the revelation of God's divine nature. We have been transformed into becoming super beings - the wonderful products of the super God. We have now had the privilege to be born of God and the opportunity to become sharers of his very nature.

> [4]***Whereby are given unto us exceeding great and precious promises: that by these ye might be partakers of the divine nature, having escaped the corruption that is in the world through lust.*** **II Peter 1:4**

Did you see the substance of the new creations in Christ? They are not ordinary beings. They are God's super creations. The new creation is something new that has come into existence. He is a master of Satan. Glory to God! That's who we are. Yes! That's who I am. I am a newly branded personality that never existed before. I am a being that is full of the ability of God. I have now become an agent of the miraculous. I am a proof producer. And so are you.

I stumbled into a story written about John G. Lake in the book, God's generals. A raging plague swept over portions of an African nation in January 1910. In less than a month, one quarter of the entire population had died. In fact, the plague was so contagious that the government offered $1,000 to any nurse who would care for the sick. Lake and his team assistants went to help, free of charge. He and one assistant would go into the house, bring out the dead, and bury them. But no symptom of the plague ever touched him.

At the height of this horrible plague, a doctor sent for Lake and asked him. "What have you been doing to protect yourself? You must have a secret!" to his Lake responded.

> *"Brother it is the law of the Spirit of life*
> *In Christ Jesus. I believe that just as long*
> *As I keep my soul in contact with the living*
> *God so that His Spirit is flowing into my*
> *Soul and body that no germ will ever attach*
> *Itself to me, for the Spirit of God will kill it."*

Lake then invited the doctor to experiment with him. He asked the doctor to take the foam from the lungs of a dead plague victim and put it under a microscope. The doctor did so and found that the germs died instantly in lake's hand. Those who witnessed the experiment stood in amazement as lake continued to give glory to God, explaining the phenomenon like this:

> *"You can fill my hand with them and*
> *I will keep it under the microscope, and*
> *Instead of these germs remaining*
> *Alive, they will die instantly."*

This same power constantly flowed though lake's hands into the bodies of the afflicted bringing healing to the masses. The "lightings of God" blasted all disease and infirmity.

These are the lightnings of God in us. It is a present day reality and our present hour possession.

At this point, I'll also like to show you a deeper truth.

> [3]***Jesus answered and said unto him, Verily, verily, I say unto thee, Except a man be born again, he cannot see the kingdom of God.*** [6]***That which is born of the flesh is flesh; and that which is born of the Spirit is spirit.*** **John 3:3 & 6.**

The born again child of God is one whose substance of being has been utterly transformed. The spirit of that person is now completely changed. The Christian is no longer human. Now take a look at that verse 6 again. Anyone born of a natural being will be a natural being but anyone born of the Spirit is spirit. Now this means that the born again believer is spirit. The believer is actually born of God. Let's look at this.

> [24]***God is a Spirit: and they that worship him must worship him in spirit and in truth.*** **John 4:24.**

God is a Spirit. He gave birth to the born again Christian. A spiritual being can never give birth to a physical being. Since God is a Spirit he would give birth to Spirit. Every child of God is Spirit. That's our normal life. We live our lives from our Spirit. We are not controlled or driven by our senses. We walk in the Spirit and by the Spirit. Our inward man is what describes us.

> [16]***For which cause we faint not; but though our outward man perish, yet the inward man is renewed day by day.*** **2 cor. 4:16;**

Our inward man is what describes the real us. We ceased to be physical beings the moment we became born again. When we became born again we were no longer the "born by my parents" kind of being. We are now totally and completely born of God.

> [4]***Ye are of God, little children, and have overcome them: because greater is he that is in you, than he that is in the world.*** **1 John 4:4**

Jesus lived like it and showed us what it meant to live like spirit. He proved that he was a master over the forces of nature when he turned water into sweet wine. He spoke to the winds and the sea and people were astonished saying what kind of a man is this, that even the winds and the sea obey him. With his Spittle and sand from the ground he healed the blind man. With five loaves of bread and two fishes about twelve thousand (5,000 men including women and children) were satisfactorily fed. He spoke to a fig tree and it dried up from its roots. A woman with the issue of blood touched the hem of his garment and was immediately healed form her infirmity. He raised a widow's son back to life. Lazarus was dead and stinking after four days but Jesus, by the ability of the Spirit, brought him back to life. He healed the epileptic boy - a dear son to his father. He cast out seven demons from Mary Magdalene. He unstopped deaf ears. He healed the sick. He raised the dead and cleansed the lepers.

This was Jesus demonstrating the abilities of the divine life to us. The divine life is absolutely limitless. Eternal life is the most potent life – whether in heaven or on earth.

> [12]***But as many as received him, to them gave he power to become the sons of God, even to them that believe on his name:*** [13]***Which were born, not of blood, nor of the will of the flesh, nor of the will of man, but of God.*** **John 1:12-13;**

Remember, I had told you previously that the born again believer is spirit. Haven seen John 1:12-13, you'll discover that anyone who receives Christ also receives the power to become a son or daughter of God. Then in verse 13, it tells us how the believers are born. It says, not of blood... How could anyone live without blood in his body. My attention was even drawn on a certain day to a scripture in Leviticus 17 verse 11 where it says, "For the life of the flesh is in the blood". So every human is supposed to have blood running in him to make him live. That means humans live on and by blood. But for the Christian, the scripture declares that they do not live by blood. This authenticates my previous point that everyone in Christ is Spirit.

When Jesus died he shed all of his blood for humanity, now don't forget that his side was pierced and blood gushed out and then water too. It was said that his heart was ruptured and this meant that all his blood gushed out. When he died, was buried and rose from the dead, there was still no blood in his body. So you could ask yourself a question then: How did he live without blood in his body?

[4]Therefore we are buried with him by baptism into death: that like as Christ was raised up from the dead by the glory of the Father, even so we also should walk in newness of life. **Romans 6:4;**

Jesus was raised from the dead, by the glory of the father. This glory of the father will not really be clear to you until you have read this next scripture.

[11]But if the Spirit of him that raised up Jesus from the dead dwell in you, he that raised up Christ from the dead shall also quicken your mortal bodies by his Spirit that dwelleth in you. **Romans 8:11;**

I hope it's much clearer now? The glory of the father was actually the Sprit of God. He supplanted the human body of Jesus. He entered his body and gave it full life. This is eternal life. The very substance of Jehovah's being. It is the very essence of the divine life. This is the same life resident in the Spirit of a believer. No disease transmitted by blood can ever bring him down. How could a child of God live with sickness? No, you couldn't live like that. His life is in you. It's working in you all the time. You were born again to be a master over diseases.

[23]Being born again, not of corruptible seed, but of incorruptible, by the word of God, which liveth and abideth for ever. **1 Peter 1:23;**

This is the substance of the born again life. You were born again, not of a corruptible seed (mortal seed or sperm). You see, the Greek word used here is the word "Sperma". This is the same word that is translated sperm – in the English dictionary. Do you know that there are millions and millions of sperm cells in the male semen and that only one sperm cell fertilizes the egg of the woman then others die? Do you also know that after fertilization and the entire gestation period, the child is born which one day will also die? But thanks to God! The seed that produced us cannot die. It is the word that brought eternal life to our Spirit. The seed of God is that living rhema of God.

[4]Ye are of God, little children, and have overcome them: because greater is he that is in you, than he that is in the world. **1 John 4:4;**

We are of God. We are holistically of God. We are truly and fully of God. The greater one came to reside in us when we were born again. We are no ordinary beings. We are more than conquerors.

[4]For whatsoever is born of God overcometh the world: and this is the victory that overcometh the world, even our faith. 1 John 5:4;

We are born of God. We are bigger than the troubles in this world. When those in the world are saying there is a casting down, we arise and say there is a lifting up for us. This is all because, in him we move, in him we live and in him we have our being.

[10]For we are his workmanship, created in Christ Jesus unto good works, which God hath before ordained that we should walk in them. **Ephesians 2:10;**

We are God's handiwork. We are his accomplishment. We are his creation (a different type of Creation). We are special beings. He is our master craftsman. He crafted us divinely and uniquely for his special purpose. So we can do unusual things for the kingdom. We are products of the supernatural, for the supernatural and by the supernatural. So we can do same works Jesus did on the earth because we have eternal life – the same life that was in Christ.

[24]Verily, verily, I say unto you, He that heareth my word, and believeth on him that sent me, hath everlasting life, and shall not come into condemnation; but is passed from death unto life. **John 5:24;**

CHAPTER THREE
DIVINE HEALTH

If you would take a second look at this topic, you might want to ask me a very intelligent question: why divine health and not healing? Now, you must understand that healing was also a part of God's plan in the work of redemption. However, if we choose to put it in that syntactical form, it could also mean that God's plan is actually to heal us today. That's true on the one hand. But there's a deeper and higher truth at this level. His truth is that God has already given to us divine health when Jesus died on the cross as our substitutionary sacrifice. He healed us then and all the sick are to do now is receive this package and live constantly in the reality of it. Isn't this just wonderful?

[8]Jesus Christ the same yesterday, and to day, and for ever. **Hebrews 13:8**

Jesus is the greatest healer ever. He was anointed by God for that purpose. He defeated sickness and the author of it both in his terrestrial sojourn and in his crucifixion. As though it wasn't enough at the cross, this awesome victory that took place in the darkest regions of hell was actually ours. When anyone identifies with Christ now, he or she becomes the master of Satan and a greater than the adversary. No wonder the bible says that the new creation in Christ will lay hands on the sick and they shall recover.

But before we go deeply into the subject of divine health, let's take a look at how sickness came into the scene.

The first man Adam was created a perfect being and in God's image and as a result, he was completely free from any form of sickness or disease. However, when he sinned against God upon his fall, he died spiritually. This spiritual death was what introduced the doorway to diseases, sicknesses and physical death which he originally or before his fall, was completely immune from. This introduction as a result of spiritual death is what Paul describes in the book of Romans to have passed unto every other generation from Adam.

> [17]***For if by one man's offence death reigned by one; much more they which receive abundance of grace and of the gift of righteousness shall reign in life by one, Jesus Christ.)*** **Roman 5:17;**

If Adam (man) had not died spiritually, access could never have been granted to sickness, diseases and death to parade themselves in such an obvious manner. When man sinned against God by heeding the devils advice, he handed over God's authority in his life to Satan. As a result of this, Satan became the god of this world. One of the dividends of his rulership was the pollution of the air with germs or microbes too small to be seen by the ordinary eye in order to afflict man with diseases and sicknesses.

Contrary to the belief of some ignorant people, sicknesses or diseases and even death are as a result of Satan's reign as the god of this world.

Sin, sickness, diseases and death and death are all works of the devil and this was the reason why Jesus came. His coming was to bring it to a conclusive end.

> [8]***... For this purpose the Son of God was manifested, that he might destroy the works of the devil.*** **1 John 3:8;**

When the father-God sent Jesus to the earth, the greater part of his ministry was characterized by the healing of the sick and oppressed. He was specially anointed by God to carry out that very unique assignment. This however goes to reveal God's ultimate plan for humanity – which is that man, would live in divine health.

> [38]***How God anointed Jesus of Nazareth with the Holy Ghost and with power: who went about doing good, and healing all that were oppressed of the devil; for God was with him.*** **Acts 10:38;**

The ministry of Jesus was completely in sync with the fathers plan. It was God's plan after diseases and sickness were introduced, to destroy the power of diseases and sicknesses and set man completely free from sufferings and pain.

> [16]*When the even was come, they brought unto him many that were possessed with devils: and he cast out the spirits with his word, and healed all that were sick:* [17]*That it might be fulfilled which was spoken by Esaias the prophet, saying, Himself took our infirmities, and bare our sicknesses.* **Mathew 8:16-17**

> [32]*And at even, when the sun did set, they brought unto him all that were diseased, and them that were possessed with devils.* [33]*And all the city was gathered together at the door.* [34]*And he healed many that were sick of divers diseases, and cast out many devils; and suffered not the devils to speak, because they knew him.* **Mark 1:32-34;**

The ministry of Jesus while he was on earth was characterized by compassion for the sick and healing for their bodies.

> [23]*And Jesus went about all Galilee, teaching in their synagogues, and preaching the gospel of the kingdom, and healing all manner of sickness and all manner of disease among the people.* [24]*And his fame went throughout all Syria: and they brought unto him all sick people that were taken with divers diseases and torments, and those which were possessed with devils, and those which were lunatick, and those that had the palsy; and he healed them.* [25]*And there followed him great multitudes of people from Galilee, and from Decapolis, and from Jerusalem, and from Judaea, and from beyond Jordan.* **Mathew 4:23-25;**

And Jesus preached the gospel of the kingdom and healed all manner of sickness and diseases among the people. I really love this part, "*all manner of sickness and all manner of diseases*". In verse 24, they brought to Jesus all sick people that had divers diseases and torments and those possessed with devils. They also brought the lunatic and those that had the palsy and he healed them all. These healing reports were so striking that in verse 25 the multitude followed him... These Testimonies simply point to the fact that this was the father's original, redemptive idea.

In the entire chapter of John 11, we also see the story of Lazarus who got so sick and died as a result. But physical death, being a consequence of the same old spiritual death was still as bad as being in the same class with sickness and diseases which were also the unmitigated consequences of spiritual death.

After Lazarus' death, Jesus proved his mastery over physical death as Lazarus rose from the dead after haven being in the grave for four days.

> ***[10]And he was teaching in one of the synagogues on the sabbath. [11]And, behold, there was a woman which had a spirit of infirmity eighteen years, and was bowed together, and could in no wise lift up herself. [12]And when Jesus saw her, he called her to him, and said unto her, Woman, thou art loosed from thine infirmity. [13]And he laid his hands on her: and immediately she was made straight, and glorified God. [14]And the ruler of the synagogue answered with indignation, because that Jesus had healed on the sabbath day, and said unto the people, There are six days in which men ought to work: in them therefore come and be healed, and not on the sabbath day. [15]The Lord then answered him, and said, Thou hypocrite, doth not each one of you on the sabbath loose his ox or his ass from the stall, and lead him away to watering? [16]And ought not this woman, being a daughter of Abraham, whom Satan hath bound, lo, these eighteen years, be loosed from this bond on the sabbath day? [17]And when he had said these things, all his adversaries were ashamed: and all the people rejoiced for all the glorious things that were done by him.*** **Luke 13:10-17**

Jesus healed the woman that was bound with the Spirit of infirmity for eighteen long years. He was heavily criticized by the keepers of the law because he had healed this woman on the Sabbath. But listen to Jesus' reply, "Ought not this woman whom Satan hath bound, lo, these eighteen years, to have been loosed from this bond on the Sabbath day?"

Now this reveals who was responsible for this physical infirmity. It was Satan. Satan had bound her with this infirmity for eighteen years but Jesus – the master healer had said to her, "woman thou art loosed from thine infirmity".

I had to present to you by the picture of the ministry of Christ that the reason for Jesus' coming was also to paralyze the painful effects of sickness and disease.

[14]Forasmuch then as the children are partakers of flesh and blood, he also himself likewise took part of the same; that through death he might destroy him that had the power of death, that is, the devil; **Heb., 2:14;**

Jesus was the word made flesh. He came to the earth to destroy him that (formerly) had the power of death that is, the devil. This victory was for us. So now we live above sin, sickness, disease and death. Hallelujah! We live above sin, sicknesses and diseases. What a wonderful life we have been born into.

[4]Surely he hath borne our griefs, and carried our sorrows: yet we did esteem him stricken, smitten of God, and afflicted. [5]But he was wounded for our transgressions, he was bruised for our iniquities: the chastisement of our peace was upon him; and with his stripes we are healed. [6]All we like sheep have gone astray; we have turned everyone to his own way; and the LORD hath laid on him the iniquity of us all. **Isaiah 53:4-6;**

It says surely he hath borne our griefs and carried our sorrows. Actually this translation that points "our griefs and sorrows" is not really correct. The originally literal translation actually reads "sicknesses and diseases". This originally, will now read *"surely he hath borne our sicknesses and carried our diseases; yet we did esteem him stricken smitten of God and afflicted"*. The interesting thing about this scripture is that this truth is a present hour reality. Christ has done it. He carried our diseases and bore our sicknesses upon his Spirit. So he became sick and diseased on the cross with our sickness and diseases. But did you know it was God who was responsible for all of these. He was stricken, smitten and afflicted of God. Can we take a look at the tenth verse?

[10]Yet it pleased the LORD to bruise him; he hath put him to grief: when thou shalt make his soul an offering for sin, he shall see his seed, he shall prolong his days, and the pleasure of the LORD shall prosper in his hand. **Isaiah 53:10;**

Now you would clearly see who was responsible for all these. It was the father. He forsook his son for a while because he was made sin. He put our sicknesses and sins upon Jesus. By this, the picture of God's redemptive plan then becomes clearer. Jesus was our substitutionary sacrifice. He is the only reason we can live above sicknesses and diseases now.

Look at verse 5, it says *he was wounded for our transgressions, he was bruised for our iniquities; the chastisement of our peace was upon him; and with his stripes we are healed.* He did not just deal with the sin problem, but also with our iniquities (the sins we did not commit but are yet suffering the consequences of). And now by the stripes given Jesus, we have been healed. Medical research has this to say, that all sicknesses and diseases are classified into thirty nine major groups. This equals the number of stripes given Jesus. So with the thirty nine stripes, the Sickness and diseases problem is completely defeated. I like what Peter later said after Jesus had died and resurrected.

> ***24Who his own self bare our sins in his own body on the tree, that we, being dead to sins, should live unto righteousness: by whose stripes ye were healed.*** **1 peter 2:24.**

It says we were healed. We are not going to or about to be healed. it's a present day reality and not a promise for another day. It's a glorious possession. And the best part is that it is ours. We have been healed. We have the license to walk completely in divine health. If he had borne our sicknesses and carried our diseases, it would not be appropriate for us to carry or bear them again. Don't you think so?

> ***13Is any among you afflicted? let him pray. Is any merry? let him sing psalms. 14Is any sick among you? let him call for the elders of the church; and let them pray over him, anointing him with oil in the name of the Lord: 15And the prayer of faith shall save the sick, and the Lord shall raise him up; and if he have committed sins, they shall be forgiven him.*** **James 5:13 – 15**

Someone might like to disprove this scriptural and higher truth by quoting this scripture in the book of James. In verse 14, it says *is any sick among you...*? Don't forget he was talking to Christians. This question should now pop-up in your mind. If Christ took our sicknesses then why should any Christian be sick?

James was talking to baby Christians. They are those who either did not know that the same way Jesus took their sins away, he also took their sicknesses and diseases or that they have not acted upon their right to live above sicknesses. This is actually what could happen to a Christian who either does not know his or her right or is not acting on it.

Healing is provided for the yet to be mature believers that why *healing is the children's bread.* But the mature in Christ know that they have a holistic and divine health and they stand on it. By his stripes we were healed.

> ***[1]And I, brethren, could not speak unto you as unto spiritual, but as unto carnal, even as unto babes in Christ. [2]I have fed you with milk, and not with meat: for hitherto ye were not able to bear it, neither yet now are ye able. [3]For ye are yet carnal: forwhereas there is among you envying, and strife, and divisions, are ye not carnal, and walk as men?*** **1 Corinthians 3:1-3;**

This is the kind of believer that has not come to a level of maturity in his walk with God. He has the life of God in him but has never taken advantage of his privilege. They are still sense-driven and walk as ordinary men. They are not filled with the word of God. They are not growing spiritually.

> ***[12]For when for the time ye ought to be teachers, ye have need that one teach you again which be the first principles of the oracles of God; and are become such as have need of milk, and not of strong meat. [13]For every one that useth milk is unskilful in the word of righteousness: for he is a babe.*** **Heb. 5:12-13;**

Babes in Christ may not be able to enjoy their full privileges and rights in Christ until they mature in the things of the spirit. The mature Christian could also be attacked by some symptoms but he or she knows enough to always declare, "Thanks to God, I have been healed more than 2000 years ago, on the cross".

> ***[16]He that believeth and is baptized shall be saved; but he that believeth not shall be damned. [17]And these signs shall follow them that believe; In my name shall they cast out devils; they shall speak with new tongues; [18]They shall take up serpents; and if they drink any deadly thing, it shall not hurt them; they shall lay hands on the sick, and they shall recover.*** **Mark 16:16-18**

Since the mature Christian can live and walk in divine health, they then have the ultimate license to impart healing to any sick body. If they lay their hands on the sick, they'll receive their healing.

> ***[20]For ye are bought with a price: therefore glorify God in your body, and in your spirit, which are God's.*** **1 Corinthians 6:20**

CHAPTER FOUR
FAITH

Faith is the ability of the Spirit of a human to respond to God's word. Now, since I said this kind of faith responds to God's word, you would now see that I couldn't be talking about the sense knowledge kind of faith is that faith that is solely dependent on the sense (touch, sight, hearing, taste and smell). Sense knowledge will always say if it's not logically based then it's not possible. Sense knowledge faith tells you that if there's no money in your pocket, you're simply broke and poor.

The God kind of faith has its own source from the word of God. This kind of faith says. "If it is in sync with the word of God then it is so". This kind of faith starts in its seed form when a believer comes into Christ.

> ***[8]For by grace are ye saved through faith; and that not of yourselves: it is the gift of God:*** **Ephesians 2:8**

This scripture says we are saved through faith. This means that faith is absolutely a necessary ingredient at salvation. Anyone who must accept Christ must first believe that he died and rose again on the third day. Now this is pivotal for the reality of the blessings of the finished work of Christ to begin to show forth in that person's life.

> ***8**But what saith it? The word is nigh thee, even in thy mouth, and in thy heart: that is, the word of faith, which we preach; **9**That if thou shalt confess with thy mouth the Lord Jesus, and shalt believe in thine heart that God hath raised him from the dead, thou shalt be saved. **10**For with the heart man believeth unto righteousness; and with the mouth confession is made unto salvation. **11**For the scripture saith, Whosoever believeth on him shall not be ashamed. **12**For there is no difference between the Jew and the Greek: for the same Lord over all is rich unto all that call upon him. **13**For whosoever shall call upon the name of the Lord shall be saved. **14**How then shall they call on him in whom they have not believed? and how shall they believe in him of whom they have not heard? and how shall they hear without a preacher?* **Romans 10:8-14;**

Christianity is not a religion. Religion is based on works but Christianity is on faith. Christianity is a divine relationship: a strong union between the believer and the father-God but religion presents the picture of a mere human being, made from the dust of the ground and absolutely unworthy of relating with the father. The religious is always trying to be close to God and perhaps never worthy to stand before him. So they believe they must do a lot of clean things so as to earn the credits of a very clean God. Christianity is not joining a church. It is not about having your sins forgiven. It is simply about receiving the life and nature of God. So how do you know you have it? When you confess Jesus as your Saviour and lord, then you have it. You don't have to feel like it before you declare, "I have it". This is the faith of God

> ***10**For as the rain cometh down, and the snow from heaven, and returneth not thither, but watereth the earth, and maketh it bring forth and bud, that it may give seed to the sower, and bread to the eater: **11**So shall my word be that goeth forth out of my mouth: it shall not return unto me void, but it shall accomplish that which I please, and it shall prosper in the thing whereto I sent it.* **Isaiah 55:10-11**

> ***12**Then said the LORD unto me, Thou hast well seen: for I will hasten my word to perform it.* **Jeremiah 1:12;**

The person of faith is one who completely believes on the integrity of God's word. God's word is the most potent force ever. But this force lives in our spirits and can be dispensed whenever we speak in consonance with these integrity-filled words. Looking at verse 10 of these afore-mentioned scriptures, it gives us a picture of rain and snow that is always released from heaven. This analysis actually concentrates on the potency of God's word. So we would say, on this premise, that God's word can be released from anywhere. It says the rain comes down and the snow from heaven. This means that the word goes in a certain direction when released and from a definite place. In that scripture, it continues by saying that the rain or snow cannot return to its source. That's peculiar to God's word, immediately it is released, it cannot return to its source. It only has one direction and it must be to the place it was directed. This is the reason why that scripture yet says, it waters the earth. The rain also causes the earth to bud. This reveals the words productive ability. No part of God's word can be said to be void.

> ***3For I say, through the grace given unto me, to every man that is among you, not to think of himself more highly than he ought to think; but to think soberly, according as God hath dealt to every man the measure of faith.*** **Romans 12:3**

Paul, speaking to the believers in Rome, affirmed that God has dealt unto every believer, the measure of faith. He didn't say a measure of faith or some measure of faith else it would have depicted varying measures. God has given every Christian the same level of faith such that no Christian can be said to be without faith. The problem with some Christians is not the issue of whether or not they have the faith but in their ability to use the faith they have. But it is the gospel truth that every Christian was given the faith of God.

> ***22But be ye doers of the word, and not hearers only, deceiving your own selves. 23For if any be a hearer of the word, and not a doer, he is like unto a man beholding his natural face in a glass: 24For he beholdeth himself, and goeth his way, and straightway forgetteth what manner of man he was.*** **James 1:22-24,**

With the faith the believer carries, he lives by the dictates and direction of God's word. He is that Christian that does not lose focus on his original image. He lives constantly with the consciousness of the picture of his life. That's precisely what the word of God is to the believer. The word shows him what he really is. The blessings of the word manifests constantly in his life because the word has become his life.

> [12]*For the word of God is quick, and powerful, and sharper than any twoedged sword, piercing even to the dividing asunder of soul and spirit, and of the joints and marrow, and is a discerner of the thoughts and intents of the heart.* **Hebrew 4:12**

We have faith and live completely by it. Little wonder Habakkuk 2:4 says that *the just shall live by his faith*. Yes! Living by faith is living by the word. The word of God is a living thing. It can grow in your spirit. It can make you whatever it says. It can reproduce the divine life to its full in our spirits. The word has the best nourishment ever for our spirit. It gives strength to us. The word is full of the power of God. It has great ability in it. It can pierce through our Spirits.

> [4]*But he answered and said, It is written, Man shall not live by bread alone, but by every word that proceedeth out of the mouth of God.* **Mathew 4:4;**

Just like the physical body needs good food and exercise to grow, the Christian needs more of God's word and the constant practice of the word to grow. There are spiritual nutrients in the word of God. These nutrients account for the glowing life of the glowing christian.

> [18]*Of his own will begat he us with the word of truth, that we should be a kind of firstfruits of his creatures.* **James 1:18**

> [23]*Being born again, not of corruptible seed, but of incorruptible, by the word of God, which liveth and abideth for ever.* **1 peter 1:23;**

This is true about every Christian. We were born by the word of truth. It is the word of God that lives and abides forever. How I love the word of God. The word, according to James, has made us a special type of God's creation. Yes! That's who we are. We are born of God and with his own very life. We are gods. We function in the same class with God. We can do what the word says we can do. We can make things happen by the agency of the working and living word in us.

> [16]*Let the word of Christ dwell in you richly in all wisdom; teaching and admonishing one another in psalms and hymns and spiritual songs, singing with grace in your hearts to the Lord.* **Colossians 3:16**

We are full of the word. The word is dominating our entire lives. It not only takes precedence in our life affairs but also gives us revelation with which we function with spiritual clarity. The word of God is the wisdom of God. With it, we do the right things expected of us by the Spirit and at the right time.

> [2]***And be not conformed to this world: but be ye transformed by the renewing of your mind, that ye may prove what is that good, and acceptable, and perfect, will of God.*** **Romans 12:2**

With the word of God in our mouth and our spirit, we get our lives completely transformed. We increase from grace to grace and from strength to strength. Our minds are constantly dominated by the word. We grow to think like God. We function like God. The divine abilities in our spirits are becoming stronger all the time. We live and function in God's will. His essence now reveals the glory of our beautiful life.

> [32]***And now, brethren, I commend you to God, and to the word of his grace, which is able to build you up, and to give you an inheritance among all them which are sanctified.*** **Acts 20:32**

The word is building our faith sense. It is the singular agent that makes us do the things that are pleasant to the father. It builds the love nature of the father in our spirits. Making us love like the father loves. We have become completely taken over by the word. The word of God rules us. It is the only food that satisfies our spiritual being.

> [7]***If ye abide in me, and my words abide in you, ye shall ask what ye will, and it shall be done unto you.*** **John 15:7**

With God's word in us, we are confident that whatever we ask of God is already done. There is no issue of unanswered prayers again. Our lives only move in the upward and forward directions. With the word in us, our relationship with the father is an absolutely strong one.

> [2]***Looking unto Jesus the author and finisher of our faith; who for the joy that was set before him endured the cross, despising the shame, and is set down at the right hand of the throne of God.*** **Hebrews 12:2**

Jesus is the author of our faith. When we became born again, our faith became fully instituted. When we confessed him as Lord and believed that he died and rose again on the third day, that very act of faith brought us into God's family – the family of Faith. Jesus is not just the author but is also the perfecter of our faith. This means that Jesus – the living word of God, is the one who stabilizes, strengthens and takes our faith to progressive levels.

> [16]***Ye have not chosen me, but I have chosen you, and ordained you, that ye should go and bring forth fruit, and that your fruit should remain: that whatsoever ye shall ask of the Father in my name, he may give it you.***
> **John 15:16;**

This is the prime reason why we know we've been chosen by God. The word says so and we believe it. We have been specially ordained to produce results. With God's word in us now we know what to produce and how to produce it.

> [20]***He sent his word, and healed them, and delivered them from their destructions.*** **Psalm 107:20;**

The word in our lips as a people of faith brings healing to the sick. The oppressed are delivered by us by the reason of the faith-filled words spoken by us. We declare to the sick and the diseased, "*With his stripes you are healed*".

> [2]***For by it[faith] the elders obtained a good report.*** **Hebrews 11:2;**

Our lives command testimonies by the reason of the faith of God resident in our Spirits. Our lives have purposefully become dependent on the living word of God. The word has shown us who we are. We are not ordinary beings. We are faith personalities.

> [7]***(For we walk by faith, not by sight:)*** **2 Corinthians. 5:7**

> [17]***So then faith cometh by hearing, and hearing by the word of God.***
> **Rom. 10:17,**

> [6]***But without faith it is impossible to please him: for he that cometh to God must believe that he is, and that he is a rewarder of them that diligently seek him.*** **Heb. 11:6;**

The word has made us faith men and women. Now we can absolutely please God. Hallelujah!

> [89]***For ever, O LORD, thy word is settled in heaven.*** **Psalm 119:89;**

CHAPTER FIVE
WISDOM

There are many great benefits that accrue to us believers. These blessings are extensive and inexhaustible. If anyone is in Christ, he is a new creation with great inheritances to enjoy. When you buy a television set for example, by default, some abilities or features come with the television set. The moment you purchase the television set, you are free to enjoy all the features that come with the television by default. That's what Christianity is like. Immediately you become born again, you stand the chance to enjoy every benefit that comes with the experience.

If there is electricity in your house and you need to turn on the lights, all you need to do is to simply use the switch and the house will be lightened up. As simply as it seems, that's how our lives should be. Our lives are already wired to function in a certain way as Christians. We use the right switch of confession and instantly the result becomes automatic in our lives.

Jesus is the wisdom of God. Wisdom has never been, and can never be a function of the reasoning facilities. It is not philosophical, psychological or metaphysical. Wisdom is not a gift for the subconscious mind. It is not a possession for intellectuals. Wisdom is the gift of God. It comes from above and as we act on the living word of God.

Sometimes when we act on God's word, we need to pause for some time and allow the spirit speak to us and give us our destiny direction. With his wisdom in us, we could never be helpless, hopeless and lacking direction.

> ***30But of him are ye in Christ Jesus, who of God is made unto us wisdom, and righteousness, and sanctification, and redemption:*** **I Corinthians 1:30**

God has made Jesus Christ our wisdom. So if we have Christ in us, we have the wisdom of God alive in our spirit. Immediately we come into Christ, wisdom becomes our spiritual asset. Jesus Christ is the expression of God's entire wisdom. He is the wisdom of God. With the wisdom of God in our spirits, we function at a high level of the divine life. Wisdom makes us know, relate with with and put God's ability to work. By the reason of God's word, everyone in Christ ought to know that wisdom is present right now in him or her. A great measure of God's divine wisdom lies in us. Wisdom could however be dormant in the life of a christian. This puts the believer at a level where he has to know that he actually has a responsibility with this dormant wisdom. We activate it whenever we put the word of God to work.

> ***4Abide in me, and I in you. As the branch cannot bear fruit of itself, except it abide in the vine; no more can ye, except ye abide in me. 5I am the vine, ye are the branches: He that abideth in me, and I in him, the same bringeth forth much fruit: for without me ye can do nothing.*** **John 15:4-5**

The divine connection we have with God is what makes us productive in life. It is that complete dependence on him. That total co-operation with the Holy Spirit. This act of working together with the spirit of God builds a strong awareness of his presence in you. And as this partnership and deep relationship continues, he communicates his mind to you every moment whenever and wherever necessary. With this constant communion with the Holy Spirit, your faculties are dominated by the abilities of the spirit and the mind of God. You will live like a super being because you have learnt to be spiritually sensitive to the voice of the spirit.

> ***26But when the Comforter is come, whom I will send unto you from the Father, even the Spirit of truth, which proceedeth from the Father, he shall testify of me:* John 15:26**

The original translation of the "spirit of truth" here is the "spirit of reality". Reality is whatever God says in his word about a particular thing. However, reality to the natural man comes from the senses. The natural man believes absolutely on what he can see, feel, smell, taste and hear. If it doesn't come through these avenues to him, then it is definitely not reality.

The spirit of reality does not communicate to the believers through the senses. He communicates Gods word which is reality to the Christian. Consequently, the Christian begins to build up his spiritual facilities into believing the voice of the spirit and not the voice of logic or his reasoning.

> ***13Howbeit when he, the Spirit of truth, is come, he will guide you into all truth: for he shall not speak of himself; but whatsoever he shall hear, that shall he speak: and he will shew you things to come. 14He shall glorify me: for he shall receive of mine, and shall shew it unto you. 15All things that the Father hath are mine: therefore said I, that he shall take of mine, and shall shew it unto you.* John 16:13-15**

The spirit of wisdom is the spirit of reality. His assignment is to transmit spiritual realities to our spirits. I had told you earlier that the natural man must engage his senses and reasoning in other to arrive at a reasonable conclusion. He looks at his wallet, checks his bank account and if there is no money, he declares "I am broke". His sight revealed to him how broke he was. But the spirit of reality will make the reality of the spirit realm real to you so that you can relate with them like the physical man handles materials things. Revelation is a function of the spirit of reality. The natural man cannot relate with God's revelation. It only takes the presence of the spirit to do that.

[5]If any of you lack wisdom, let him ask of God, that giveth to all men liberally, and upbraideth not; and it shall be given him. **James 1:5**

This is the description of wisdom by the babe in Christ Jesus. The book of James was actually writing to spiritual babes – those who could not relate with spiritual realities. Let's take a look at their conversation *"if anyone lacks wisdom..."* How could the Christian ever lack wisdom? The book of I Corinthians 1:30, says that Christ has been made unto us wisdom, sanctification, righteousness and redemption. Since Jesus is my wisdom and I have accepted him as my savior and Lord, then I can boldly declare "I have the wisdom of God in me".

God's ultimate redemption plan is based on absolute faith. How does faith come then? It comes by the word of God. No wonder the bible is the word of faith. Faith is simply acting upon the word of God. Therefore if Jesus has been made wisdom unto us we should simply claim it and enjoy this possession by faith. This then proves that as a believer, you can never lack the wisdom of God.

[15]For this reason, because I have heard of your faith in the Lord Jesus and your love toward all the saints (the people of God), [16]I do not cease to give thanks for you, making mention of you in my prayers. [17][For I always pray to] the God of our Lord Jesus Christ, the Father of glory, that He may grant you a spirit of wisdom and revelation [of insight into mysteries and secrets] in the [deep and intimate] knowledge of Him,[18]By having the eyes of your heart flooded with light, so that you can know and understand the hope to which He has called you, and how rich is His glorious inheritance in the saints (His set-apart ones), [19]And [so that you can know and understand] what is the immeasurable and unlimited and surpassing greatness of His power in and for us who believe, as demonstrated in the working of His mighty strength, [20]Which He exerted in Christ when He raised Him from the dead and seated Him at His [own] right hand in the heavenly [places], [21]Far above all rule and authority and power and dominion and every name that is named [above every title that can be conferred], not only in this age and in this world, but also in the age and the world which are to come. [22]And He has put all things under His feet and has appointed Him the universal and supreme Head of the church [a headship exercised throughout the church], [23]Which is His body, the fullness of Him Who fills all in all [for in that body lives the full measure of Him Who makes everything complete, and Who fills everything everywhere with Himself]. **Ephesians 1: 15-23; AMP**

Nobody can ever get wisdom from any material or human source. Wisdom cannot be gotten from an academic book or a school. Wisdom comes from our spirit.
Man is a spirit. He is in the same class with God because God is also spirit. You must know that even though man has a soul and lives in a body, the only part of man that can contact God is his spirit. That's the real man. Wisdom is absolutely a product of the spirit and not the senses or the reasoning faculties.

> ***3Blessed be the God and Father of our Lord Jesus Christ, who hath blessed us with all spiritual blessings in heavenly places in Christ:*** **Ephesians 1:3**

The Christian is different. The Christian is blessed with every spiritual blessing. Wisdom is one of these blessings. We could continually rejoice because we have deep supernatural insight into mysteries and secrets. We have the person of God's wisdom in us. The whole version of God's wisdom is now terbanacled in us. We function in wisdom. It is alive in our spirit.

> ***42The queen of the south shall rise up in the judgment with this generation, and shall condemn it: for she came from the uttermost parts of the earth to hear the wisdom of Solomon; and, behold, a greater than Solomon is here.*** **Matthew 12:42**

God gave Solomon wisdom, so much so, that his wisdom even surpassed the wisdom of the Egyptians. It was said about him that he was wiser than the wisest of men because of the wisdom given to him. His greatness was a function of the wisdom given to him. But in the case of Jesus Christ it was absolutely different. He was not given wisdom because he is the wisdom of God. When we accepted Christ as our Lord and Saviour, Jesus automatically became our wisdom. No wonder Jesus said about himself that a greater than Solomon has emerged. Since he has the personality of wisdom resident in us, then imagine how wonderful it is to be able to relate with this glorious blessing of the New Testament. In Christ, wisdom is our birthright. It's our inheritance. It is our present right. We are legal partakers of the wisdom of God.

Some might choose to disagree to the truth that every believer has the wisdom of God. But their stand point is only predicated on the fact that they might have not seen themselves demonstrating it. It's simply because they either don't know that they have it or have not taken full responsibility to use that wisdom. This truth is something we have to realize that wisdom belongs to us. We just use it whenever the need arises.

> [8]***This book of the law shall not depart out of thy mouth; but thou shalt meditate therein day and night, that thou mayest observe to do according to all that is written therein: for then thou shalt make thy way prosperous, and then thou shalt have good success.*** **Joshua 1:8**

The wisdom of God flows mostly whenever we cultivate the conscious habit of meditating in the word of God. When the word comes alive in your spirit in the place of meditation, then your life is sure to be the true definition of success.
The habit of meditation is pivotal to the constant flow of the practical wisdom of God in the life of a believer. As you meditate on the word, the *rhema* of God becomes real to your spirit. You live the word and the word in turn becomes you.
A life full of meditation is a life of glory. We become whatever we meditate on.
With God's wisdom, we walk in prosperity. With divine wisdom we know the way to the top. The secret of God has been committed to us. We now walk by the direction of the Holy Spirit. We know the deep things of God by this same spirit of wisdom.

It is very necessary or us to live in the realm of wisdom. This is very possible when we choose to constantly develop our spirit man. As children of God, we have the life of God. His nature has become resident in us. Our personality therefore has been affected by this life. We have now become one with God. We have now mingled with the wisdom of God. We now have a great force in our spirit that makes us constantly rule in this world.

> [1]***I am the true vine, and my Father is the husbandman.*** **John 15:1**

The same life present in the vine is the same life that flows in the branches. Thus, if Jesus is the wisdom of God and he is the vine, we – the branches are also carriers of the same life. The abilities in Christ have been imparted to our spirit. His omnipotence now works in our very being. His strength is now our strength.

> [13]***I can do all things through Christ which strengtheneth me.*** **Philippians 4:13**

Our constant fellowship with the father is the sure basis for a continuous manifestation of the life of God's wisdom in us. We have to grow in the things of God. We have to live with the word. Wisdom is the ability of God in the life of the believer. It is God's working power in the Christian.

> 20***Now unto him that is able to do exceeding abundantly above all that we ask or think, according to the power that worketh in us,*** **Ephesians 3:20.**

CHAPTER SIX

RIGHTEOUSNESS

The subject of righteousness is as interesting as looking into the fall of the first man Adam. Adam was created by God as an eternal being and God's crowned creation. He had God's kind of knowledge in its full light. However, his choosing to disobey God was a personal decision. He could have also chosen to obey because he had the ability to do so.

As a result of this, man became spiritually dead and unable to live in the realm of God's divine nature. This grave problem made it imperative for God to consider the possibility of imparting his own very life and nature into that spiritually dead man. Man had become a child of Satan as a result of Adam's fall but now must become a child of God if he can only receive God's nature of righteousness.
God's bestowing of man his very righteousness would now be predicated upon these vital facts.

God must handle the transgression of man legally. This means that man must be made to pay the full penalty for his sin.

> [18]***For the wrath of God is revealed from heaven against all ungodliness and unrighteousness of men, who hold the truth in unrighteousness;*** **ROMANS 1:18;**

[9]What then? are we better than they? No, in no wise: for we have before proved both Jews and Gentiles, that they are all under sin;

> [10]***As it is written, There is none righteous, no, not one:*** **ROMANS 3:9-10**

> [16]***And not as it was by one that sinned, so is the gift: for the judgment was by one to condemnation, but the free gift is of many offences unto justification.*** [17]***For if by one man's offence death reigned by one; much more they which receive abundance of grace and of the gift of righteousness shall reign in life by one, Jesus Christ.)*** [18]***Therefore as by the offence of one judgment came upon all men to condemnation; even so by the righteousness of one the free gift came upon all men unto justification of life.*** [19]***For as by one man's disobedience many were made sinners, so by the obedience of one shall many be made righteous.*** **ROMANS 5:16-19**

> [36]***He that believeth on the Son hath everlasting life: and he that believeth not the Son shall not see life; but the wrath of God abideth on him.*** **JOHN 3:36;**

Secondly, upon the sin of Adam, he gave the authority and rulership which God bestowed on him to Satan. So Satan became man's master as a result. This implies that if man must be freed from Satan's hold, it must be on legal grounds.

[34]Jesus answered them, Verily, verily, I say unto you, Whosoever committeth sin is the servant of sin. **JOHN 8:34;**

[2]Wherein in time past ye walked according to the course of this world, according to the prince of the power of the air, the spirit that now worketh in the children of disobedience: [3]Among whom also we all had our conversation in times past in the lusts of our flesh, fulfilling the desires of the flesh and of the mind; and were by nature the children of wrath, even as others. **EPHESIANS 2:2-3**

[13]Who hath delivered us from the power of darkness, and hath translated us into the kingdom of his dear Son: **COLOSSIANS 1:13**

[14]Forasmuch then as the children are partakers of flesh and blood, he also himself likewise took part of the same; that through death he might destroy him that had the power of death, that is, the devil; [15]And deliver them who through fear of death were all their lifetime subject to bondage. **HEBREWS 2:14-15.**

With respect to the nature of divinity which man lost when he fell in the garden, Satan has used the weapon of the feeling of inadequacy to hinder the relationship between man and God. That's the reason some people never feel clean. They always have the mentality of I am dirty. This feeling of unworthiness is the offshoot of a prevailing sin consciousness.

Sin consciousness is the product of the ignorance of the substitutionary work of Christ. As surprising as it may seem, many churches have cultivated the attitude of preaching sin instead of righteousness in their bid to build the people in a so-called "Holy life". They have not preached the good news that sin is no longer a problem or our problem (it has been dealt with already on the cross). It is a good news that we have become the righteousness of God in Christ. We have been redeemed from sin's captivity. We are now actual sons of God.

[2]Beloved, now are we the sons of God... **1 John 3:2,**

God's supreme plan can be boldly seen when he sent his son to die as a substitutionary sacrifice. The beautiful reality in this is that he became us, so that we might become him. He became sin so that we might become righteous. We can boldly proclaim now that we are righteous.

> *[21]For he hath made him to be sin for us, who knew no sin; that we might be made the righteousness of God in him.* **2 Corinthians 5:21,**

Righteousness does not necessarily mean right living as some people might put it. Trying to live right would be tantamount to a demonstration of works – an input by your efforts. Righteousness is received solely by faith. It is the ability to stand in the father's presence without any feeling of guilt, inferiority or condemnation. So we don't feel like sinners because we know God has made us righteous.

> *[1]There is therefore now no condemnation to them which are in Christ Jesus, who walk not after the flesh, but after the Spirit.* **Romans 8:1;**

If man had tried to be righteous all by himself after the fall of Adam, how could he ever make himself clean or worthy to stand in God's presence? It could never be possible. This was the reason for the substitutionary work of Christ. He has made us righteous.

> *[21]But now the righteousness of God without the law is manifested, being witnessed by the law and the prophets; [22]Even the righteousness of God which is by faith of Jesus Christ unto all and upon all them that believe: for there is no difference: [26]To declare, I say, at this time his righteousness: that he might be just, and the justifier of him which believeth in Jesus.* **Romans 3:21-22&26;**

Man was far from God, both in relationship and fellowship. It was difficult for man to be a sharer of God's nature. Little wonder David recounted his weaknesses in Psalms 51 when he put it to God that he had been shapen in iniquity and conceived in sin. Righteousness was not revealed in the Old Testament. That was the reason why God declared to them that the best they could be in trying to be righteous was to be unclean.

> *[6]But we are all as an unclean thing, and all our righteousnesses are as filthy rags; and we all do fade as a leaf; and our iniquities, like the wind, have taken us away.* **Isaiah 64:6;**

So since man could not be righteous by himself, God sent his son to bring his plan of making man righteous, a reality. Righteousness therefore is as free as any gift anyone can think of. It is completely God's gift to us. So our task is to simply receive and believe we have it.

> [17]*For if by one man's offence death reigned by one; much more they which receive abundance of grace and of the gift of righteousness shall reign in life by one, Jesus Christ.)* **Romans 5:17;**

In the Old Testament, God had earlier spoken about a time when this nature of righteousness would be given. It was a function of his fully resident spirit or nature in man. With this superior nature, there couldn't be a level of reasoning that we are filthy, unholy and unrighteous set of people.

When the believer understands the reality of the new creation and what we have now received as a result, sin consciousness will be defeated. The new creation is a different type of being with the very life and nature of God. The new creation functions in God's class.

The righteous believer can therefore relate and fellowship with God without feeling condemned. What a glorious life that is. We are no longer under Satan's dominion or with his nature. Through our faith in the finished work of Christ, we have discovered and received God's righteousness. For anyone who accepts Jesus as his personal Lord and Saviour, righteousness is his present hour possession.

> [17]*No weapon that is formed against thee shall prosper; and every tongue that shall rise against thee in judgment thou shalt condemn. This is the heritage of the servants of the LORD, and their righteousness is of me, saith the LORD.* **Isaiah 54:17;**

God had made Jesus sin with our sins on the cross. When Jesus put sin away thereby fulfilling the claims of justice, God could now raise him from the dead. He was made alive in the spirit by God after the problem of sin had been completely dealt with. He then became the recreated Christ. He was now the first born from the dead. God imparted his very life into that lifeless body by the Holy Ghost. He was now a new creation, completely justified by the spirit because the work of redemption was completed.

[25]Who was delivered for our offences, and was raised again for our justification. **Romans 4:25;**

God would no longer be angry with his children. God would no longer condemn them or prove them to be unworthy. The believer then should not function with an inferior mentality. There is absolutely nothing separating us from God now. No barriers, veils or walls of partition. We can now relate with God like the father would his son. We have been justified freely by faith. We have come to a place of liberty. We have perfect peace to relate with our God.

[1]Therefore being justified by faith, we have peace with God through our Lord Jesus Christ: **Romans 5:1;**

We have been declared righteous. We are the righteousness of God in Christ. We should always learn to declare this boldly before Satan. He fears these kinds of confessions because he is aware, it actually happened.

[14]Be ye not unequally yoked together with unbelievers: for what fellowship hath righteousness with unrighteousness? And what communion hath light with darkness? **2 Corinthians 6:14;**

Paul was talking to Christians in this context. He first tells them not to be yoked together with unbelievers. Then he goes ahead to say what fellowship hath righteousness with unrighteousness. This is a succinct revelation that the believer is righteousness. That's who the Christian is: the very righteousness of God.

[9]But ye are a chosen generation, a royal priesthood, an holy nation, a peculiar people; that ye should shew forth the praises of him who hath called you out of darkness into his marvellous light; **1 Peter 2:9;**

Peter was talking to Christians. I love the way he asserted that you are a holy nation. He didn't say God was going to make them a holy nation neither did he ask them to spend time praying for it. These supposed actions are good but not necessary because it would seem like you trying to become what you already are. We have been freed from unrighteousness. To enjoy this liberty continuously is to keep declaring it.

[1]Stand fast therefore in the liberty wherewith Christ hath made us free, and be not entangled again with the yoke of bondage. **Galatians 5:1;**

Isn't this beautiful? It says we should remain unshaken in this liberty. The liberty from the dominion of sin. We live above it because we lost that sinful nature in Christ. Then it says that Christ has already made us free. It is a complete deliverance from that death-doomed nature. It is a total freedom that has been given to us from the pangs of guilt. What a perfect redemption from the level of inferiority.

14For as many as are led by the Spirit of God, they are the sons of God.
15For ye have not received the spirit of bondage again to fear; but ye have received the Spirit of adoption, whereby we cry, Abba, Father. 16The Spirit itself beareth witness with our spirit, that we are the children of God:
17And if children, then heirs; heirs of God, and joint-heirs with Christ; if so be that we suffer with him, that we may be also glorified together. **Romans 8:14-17;**

By this nature of righteousness which we have, we know we are the children of God. We live with the same abilities in God by the Holy Ghost. We are bonafide heirs of God. We are joint-heirs with Christ. This is just wonderful. All i can say is thank you father for this marvelous inheritance.
We can now rejoice because of our current state. We have come into a place of reality. It's the reality that we have been completely delivered from the dominion of Satan. The penalty of our sin that justice demanded has been condemned again. We have been acquitted and discharged.

17And the work of righteousness shall be peace; and the effect of righteousness quietness and assurance forever. **Isaiah 32:17;**

Righteousness is God's nature and it is working in the life of the believer. The product of righteousness is peace. It is a peace with God to fellowship with him. However, there is another beautiful part to it. It is the effect of righteousness. The effect of righteousness is quietness and confidence forever. That means that nothing can make you feel undeserving any longer. Not even Satan.

6In his days Judah shall be saved, and Israel shall dwell safely: and this is his name whereby he shall be called, THE LORD OUR RIGHTEOUSNESS. **Jeremiah 23:6;**

[16]In those days shall Judah be saved, and Jerusalem shall dwell safely: and this is the name wherewith she shall be called, The LORD our righteousness. **Jeremiah 33:16;**

This was a promise given that was to be fulfilled in the New Testament. It is now sweet to know that we are the fulfillment of that awesome, scripture.

[16]Let us therefore come boldly unto the throne of grace, that we may obtain mercy, and find grace to help in time of need. **Hebrew 4:16;**

For this reason, we can now come boldly to the very presence of God. We come boldly because we have become exact partakers of the glory in his presence. We have been qualified to fellowship with him. We now have that divine ability. We live continuously in his presence without the feeling of inferiority, guilt and condemnation.

We are God's elect. We are more than conquerors because we are carriers of life and nature of God.

[31]What shall we then say to these things? If God be for us, who can be against us? [32]He that spared not his own Son, but delivered him up for us all, how shall he not with him also freely give us all things? [33]Who shall lay anything to the charge of God's elect? It is God that justifieth. **Romans 8:31-33;**

CHAPTER SEVEN
THE DIVINE PRESENCE

One of the most glorious possessions we have in Christ is God's divine presence in us. The revelation of God presence in the life of a believer is more precious than the best of pearls. There is a beautiful process associated with how we got to the stage where God now indwells humanity.

There was a phase in the Old Testament where God declared that Israel was his firstborn. The profits were so obvious such that it was unheard of that Israel would engage in any battle and loose out except where there was an issue within. This is the phase I call the God for us phase. God was for them so no one or nation could stand against them and prevail. The New Testament also had this to say about this phase.

> [31]***What shall we then say to these things? If God be for us, who can be against us?*** **Romans 8:31;**

This simply depicts that in this phase, the father God was in charge and for the Israelites. As the times and seasons continued to unfold, another phase was introduced.

> [23]***Behold, a virgin shall be with child, and shall bring forth a son, and they shall call his name Emmanuel, which being interpreted is, God with us.*** **Matthew 1:23;**

This is the stage of God with us. That was the phase when Jesus was in charge on the earth. He was Emmanuel – God with us. He was one personality in the Godhead that God the father sent to be with us.
The third phase is that which I call the phase of God in us.

> [49]***And, behold, I send the promise of my Father upon you: but tarry ye in the city of Jerusalem, until ye be endued with power from on high.*** **Luke 24:49;**

> [1]***And when the day of Pentecost was fully come, they were all with one accord in one place.*** [2]***And suddenly there came a sound from heaven as of a rushing mighty wind, and it filled all the house where they were sitting.*** [3]***And there appeared unto them cloven tongues like as of fire, and it sat upon each of them.*** [4]***And they were all filled with the Holy Ghost, and began to speak with other tongues, as the Spirit gave them utterance.***

Acts 2:1-4;

This was a phase in which the Holy Spirit was to be in charge. It is that phase called the "God in us" phase. The Holy Spirit would now indwell us. He would now make our lives his permanent abode.

I would like to draw your attention to the fact that man is a spirit. However, the only reason why man is the only spirit that can function effectively in this material realm is because man has a physical body. The physical body of man is the house in which the real man lives.

To this end, no spirit without a body can effectively function in this physical and mental realm. This is the sole reason why even evil spirits would always look for a body to indwell in order to function in this material realm. This was also God's plan – the plan to completely indwell man so that man would completely function like him.

> ***[14]Be ye not unequally yoked together with unbelievers: for what fellowship hath righteousness with unrighteousness? and what communion hath light with darkness? [15]And what concord hath Christ with Belial? or what part hath he that believeth with an infidel? [16]And what agreement hath the temple of God with idols? for ye are the temple of the living God; as God hath said, I will dwell in them, and walk in them; and I will be their God, and they shall be my people.*** **2 Corinthians 6:14-16**

A temple is any place where a deity is adored, revered and worshipped. But the scripture tells us that we are the temple of the living God. The presence of deity is dominant in every temple. So if the scripture shows us how that we are God's temple, then the presence of God is real in us. To this end, it will be in full order to say that every believer is a depot of God's tangible presence. It is not an experience which we aspire to achieve. This is God's ultimate plan. It is the plan to produce a very unique breed of people with his very supernatural life. With this very life, it is now very evident that we can now function in God's class. That reveals what we have become. The entirety of divinity has now been encapsulated in humanity. What glorious life. A life which is beyond this physical, sensual and mental realm.

30I and my Father are one. 31Then the Jews took up stones again to stone him. **John 10:30-31**

Oh what a wonder! This is absolutely one of the greatest revelations of the new creation. We have become one with deity. We are not ordinary, human or natural beings; we share this in his nature and life. It is now common for us to exude the powers in that very life. We are eternal beings on a foreign mission. We have been sent to function in this terrestrial sphere. As we function as ambassadors of eternity, it is common for us to display or demonstrate the lifestyle of our home. The world is our constituency. We work the works of God in this world. They see the life of God in us and through us when we lay our hands on the sick and cast out devils. These are infallible proofs that we are God's. We are offshoots of the most high.

3According as his divine power hath given unto us all things that pertain unto life and godliness, through the knowledge of him that hath called us to glory and virtue: 4Whereby are given unto us exceeding great and precious promises: that by these ye might be partakers of the divine nature, having escaped the corruption that is in the world through lust. **II Peter 1:3-4;**

By our union with God when we gave our lives to Christ, we became joint participators of his divine life. If we can only live with this consciousness as believers, our communication with the father will be strengthened and to our ministry to the world, sharpened. We have now become carriers of God's nature. We are now associates of divinity. We can now function like God because we carry his very essence in us.

When we live with the consciousness of God's indwelling presence, God will do big things through us. When we have the awareness that we are God's address, we would always win in the face of challenges. We would always declare, *"He lives in me, and greater is the one in me than any other force militating against me"*. You can also declare, *"I can do all things through Christ…* "Since God lives in us, we are custodians of his most potent abilities. His strength has become our strength. We now live a life full of dominion. Yes, we are connected to the vine. He is the vine. We have no limitation. We have now been endowed with God's limitless ability. I can do what he says I can do. I know who I am. I am who he says I am.

> *[13]For it is God which worketh in you both to will and to do of his good pleasure.* **Philippians 2:13**

We are God's factory. We are the department in which he functions. He functions in us, from us and through us. God is always doing great things on our inside. He is building strength in us. God is always doing great things on our inside. He is building strength in us. He is communicating the next set of ideas to our spirit. Isn't this wonderful to know that now we don't belong to the common order of beings? What interests me the most in this scripture is that it tells you where God works. It says, He works in us. This is a clear indication that God is terbanacled in us. We are his permanent abode. He is in us, programming us to choose and work out his good pleasures. He is the craftsman and we are the craft (handiwork).

> *[10]For we are his workmanship, created in Christ Jesus unto good works, which God hath before ordained that we should walk in them.* **Ephesians 2:10**

We have been brought into existence to function from a higher realm. We were born with a different kind of life. We are a different kind of species. We do not function or live by blood but by the spirit and the word of God.

> *[13]Which were born, not of blood, nor of the will of the flesh, nor of the will of man, but of God.* **John 1:13**

His life is our life. His ability is our ability. His strength is our strength. His wisdom is our wisdom. His righteousness is our righteousness. These are the truth we boldly confess to authenticate the reality of our divine life.
In the consciousness of the indwelling presence of God, we now live the triumphant Christian life. With God in us, we have become more than conquerors.

> *[4]Ye are of God, little children, and have overcome them: because greater is he that is in you, than he that is in the world.* **1 John 4:4**

The greater one indwells us. Our lives have become God's control room. Owing to this fact, we reign in this material realm. We live from the top and demonstrate the reality of the almighty choosing to make man his super abode.

> [27]***To whom God would make known what is the riches of the glory of this mystery among the Gentiles; which is Christ in you, the hope of glory:*** **Colossians 1:27**

Another amazing truth about the believer is that Jesus also dwells in him. This scripture brings you into the full picture of who indwells the born again child of God. It says, *"Christ in you..."* This experience is not a mystery to the believer. It can only startle the unbeliever. When we became born again, Christ began living in us. We have now become living epistles. We showcase the proofs of Christ in us when we do the works of Christ in our spheres of contact. Our lives would always produce glory. It is the glory of the risen Christ. We have passed from death to life. We then live as Christ's representatives. Of course, he produces the glory the world always wanted to see through us. We are now carriers of the eternal life.

> [20]***According to my earnest expectation and my hope, that in nothing I shall be ashamed, but that with all boldness, as always, so now also Christ shall be magnified in my body, whether it be by life, or by death.*** [21]***For to me to live is Christ, and to die is gain.*** **Philippians 1:20-21**

Paul was completely aware of the indwelling presence of Christ. He revealed it when he said: that Christ may be magnified in my body.

> [20]***I am crucified with Christ: nevertheless I live; yet not I, but Christ liveth in me: and the life which I now live in the flesh I live by the faith of the Son of God, who loved me, and gave himself for me.*** **Galatians 2:20**

This is a potent truth. Christ lives in us. I believe this truth completely. I hope you do too?

> [19]***What? know ye not that your body is the temple of the Holy Ghost which is in you, which ye have of God, and ye are not your own?*** **1 Corinthians 6:19**

It is also true in the New Testament, that the Christian is indwelt by the Holy Spirit. Some Christians are not fully aware of this. Ignorance of this truth could however open the Christian to a life of defeat. But it is wonderful for the Christian to know that the presence of the Holy Spirit is real in us. His ministry in us is now made manifest as we walk in the consciousness of this truth and fellowship with the spirit. As we commune with the spirit, he unveils to us the mind of the father. He reveals Jesus to us. He makes the presence of Jesus real to us.

> [19]***But when they deliver you up, take no thought how or what ye shall speak: for it shall be given you in that same hour what ye shall speak.***
> [20]***For it is not ye that speak, but the Spirit of your Father which speaketh in you.*** **Matthew 10:19-20;**

The spirit speaks through us whenever we speak the words of God. He lives in us and will communicate through us, what God is saying at any particular hour. With the spirit now in us, we know the father's mind and will accurately function in the father's will.

The Holy Spirit's desire is to carry out his ministry in us and through us. It is therefore our utmost responsibility to let him loose from our inside. We must give him his freedom. We have to seek opportunities for the power of the spirit to be demonstrated. And of course, when the Holy Spirit sees any opportunity to reveal the miraculous, he would always take us over.

Just like some spiritists would yield themselves to be used of evil spirit and as such be taken over by these spirits, so also we could yield to the Holy Spirit and the signs would follow.

> [29]***Whereunto I also labour, striving according to his working, which worketh in me mightily.*** **Colossians 1:29**

Paul was aware of the ongoing work of the Spirit in his life. He lived in the consciousness of the fact that God was working in him. He knew he had the intercessor working in him and producing groanings which cannot be uttered in articulate speech. He was aware that the spirit of reality was terbanacled in him. He knew that the greater one now resided in him. He knew that the same spirit which raised Christ from the dead now lives in him. This is the mindset of the spiritual believer.

> *[20]Now unto him that is able to do exceeding abundantly above all that we ask or think, according to the power that worketh in us,* Ephesians 3:20

God is able to do things beyond the comprehension of humanity but that must be in sync with the ability at work in the spirit of the believer. There are potent forces in the Christian. If these potent forces are released, unquantifiable things will begin to take place. The greatest wonder ever lies in us. The father resides in us. Jesus has his home in us. The Holy Spirit is terbanacled in us. Nothing could be greater than these.

> *[1]There is therefore now no condemnation to them which are in Christ Jesus, who walk not after the flesh, but after the Spirit.* Roman 8:1

CHAPTER EIGHT
ABILITY TO USE HIS NAME

What a joy it will be for the person who is in Christ to know that he or she has the ability to use the name of Jesus. Knowing this truth is vital for every believer. It causes the Christian to walk in this world as a person of authority. In fact, it is a reality that the Christian is a person of power. This follows the truth that the Lordship of Christ is now a working reality not only in the life of the believer but also through the pulsating life of the new creation.

On the grounds of redemption, when a person receives Christ into his life that person becomes a new creation in his spirit. At this point, spiritual death is completely annihilated from his spirit and he is no longer under the authority of Satan and the dominion of death.

> [13]*Who hath delivered us from the power of darkness, and hath translated us into the kingdom of his dear Son:* **Colossians 1:13**

The new creation has the life of God imparted into his spirit. He is born of God.

> ***[1]Whosoever believeth that Jesus is the Christ is born of God: and every one that loveth him that begat loveth him also that is begotten of him. [2]By this we know that we love the children of God, when we love God, and keep his commandments. [3]For this is the love of God, that we keep his commandments: and his commandments are not grievous. [4]For whatsoever is born of God overcometh the world: and this is the victory that overcometh the world, even our faith. [5]Who is he that overcometh the world, but he that believeth that Jesus is the Son of God? [6]This is he that came by water and blood, even Jesus Christ; not by water only, but by water and blood. And it is the Spirit that beareth witness, because the Spirit is truth. [7]For there are three that bear record in heaven, the Father, the Word, and the Holy Ghost: and these three are one. [8]And there are three that bear witness in earth, the Spirit, and the water, and the blood: and these three agree in one. [9]If we receive the witness of men, the witness of God is greater: for this is the witness of God which he hath testified of his Son. [10]He that believeth on the Son of God hath the witness***

in himself: he that believeth not God hath made him a liar; because he believeth not the record that God gave of his Son. [11]And this is the record, that God hath given to us eternal life, and this life is in his Son. [12]He that hath the Son hath life; and he that hath not the Son of God hath not life.
I John 5:1-12;

[17]Therefore if any man be in Christ, he is a new creature: old things are passed away; behold, all things are become new. **II Corinthians 5:17**

[16]The Spirit itself beareth witness with our spirit, that we are the children of God: [17]And if children, then heirs; heirs of God, and joint-heirs with Christ; if so be that we suffer with him, that we may be also glorified together. **Romans 8:16-17**

It is a salient reality that we have been delivered from Satan's authority. However, we are still in this world ruled by Satan.

[4]In whom the god of this world hath blinded the minds of them which believe not, lest the light of the glorious gospel of Christ, who is the image of God, should shine unto them. **II Corinthians 4:4,**

[2]Wherein in time past ye walked according to the course of this world, according to the prince of the power of the air, the spirit that now worketh in the children of disobedience: **Ephesians 2:2**

In these scriptures, we see that Satan is referred to as god of this world. He is also called, the prince of the power of the air.
It is a fact that Satan and his hordes can attack the child of God through trials and temptations. This is done in an attempt to destroy our fellowship with the father and deprive us of our usefulness in the service of God.

It is because of this that God has given us a potent weapon with which we would be able to counter the operations of Satan. This weapon is the name of Jesus.
The name of Jesus has so much authority vested in it. He inherited this name by conquests. This was a great achievement to God-the father and to us Christians. When he came out victorious in these conquests, he had his great name conferred on him.

[2]Hath in these last days spoken unto us by his Son, whom he hath appointed heir of all things, by whom also he made the worlds; [3]Who being the brightness of his glory, and the express image of his person, and upholding all things by the word of his power, when he had by himself purged our sins, sat down on the right hand of the Majesty on high: [4]Being made so much better than the angels, as he hath by inheritance obtained a more excellent name than they. **Hebrew 1:2 – 4**

Jesus, the very image of the father's substance inherited his name from the father. The implication now is that the power of this name can only be measured by the power of God.

I had earlier brought it to your notice, how that Jesus had acquired his name by conquests.

[15]And having spoiled principalities and powers, he made a shew of them openly, triumphing over them in it. **Colossians 2:15**

Jesus secured a tremendous victory over the hosts of darkness when he engaged them in a severe combat. He put off principalities and powers from himself. After having secured this ultimate victory on our behalf, it was very clear that he had fulfilled the demands of justice and this paved way for the reality of man's redemption.

[14]Forasmuch then as the children are partakers of flesh and blood, he also himself likewise took part of the same; that through death he might destroy him that had the power of death, that is, the devil; **Hebrews 2:14**

He did all of these before he rose from the dead. Little wonder he described the evidence of this amazing victory in his own very words in this scripture.

[18]I am he that liveth, and was dead; and, behold, I am alive for evermore, Amen; and have the keys of hell and of death. **Revelation 1:18**

Jesus completely outwitted and defeated the devil. He took from him the keys of death and hell. It was significantly evident that Jesus was an undisputed victor in this unforgettable conquest. He conquered Satan and came out from the dark regions of hell, triumphantly. Little wonder, he made a remarkable statement in Matthew 28.

[18]And Jesus came and spake unto them, saying, All power is given unto me in heaven and in earth. **Matthew 28:18**

So then, all authority over Satan and his works is vested in that name. The greatness of that name is therefore, absolutely inexhaustible.

The name was conferred upon him. This could be seen like the case of an award to be given to the one who was qualified to receive it. When Jesus therefore played his part in bringing the redemptive plan to bear, God had no choice but to confer on him the greatest award.

[9]Wherefore God also hath highly exalted him, and given him a name which is above every name: [10]That at the name of Jesus every knee should bow, of things in heaven, and things in earth, and things under the earth; **Philippians 2:9-10**

Another question could spring up from within us. It is the question of to whom the use of this name was given. Jesus inherited and had this name conferred on him after he resurrected from the dead.

[33]God hath fulfilled the same unto us their children, in that he hath raised up Jesus again; as it is also written in the second psalm, Thou art my Son, this day have I begotten thee. **Acts 13:33**

Since the resurrection of Jesus till now, that is more than two thousand years now, Jesus has been at the right hand of the father. From all indication and in his present ministry, it is evident that Jesus never needed to use this name. He was equal with God and upheld all things by the word of his power. Jesus acquired that name for the church to use it. It is the Christians that need the name in other to live above the dominion of Satan.

As a result of this ultimate victory by Jesus over Satan, we have the right to use the name of Jesus. Whether it is in our petitions, praises or even against Satan's schemes, the ever potent name of Jesus is now at our disposal for guaranteed victory.

[16]Ye have not chosen me, but I have chosen you, and ordained you, that ye should go and bring forth fruit, and that your fruit should remain: that whatsoever ye shall ask of the Father in my name, he may give it you.
John 15:16

As Christians, we should know that Jesus has given to us the power of Attorney to use his name. Whenever we use the name of Jesus in our petitions it is as good as done. So we can go ahead and talk like we already have that thing we asked for in the name of Jesus.

[12]Verily, verily, I say unto you, He that believeth on me, the works that I do shall he do also; and greater works than these shall he do; because I go unto my Father. [13]And whatsoever ye shall ask in my name, that will I do, that the Father may be glorified in the Son. [14]If ye shall ask any thing in my name, I will do it. **John 14:12-14**

This reveals to us the potency and ability in the name of Jesus. He reveals to us that with the use of his name we can multiply his works i.e. do greater things. This is true because he could only be at one place at a certain time but now, upon redemption, all who have received Christ have the ability to multiply his works in their sphere of contact.

[23]And in that day ye shall ask me nothing. Verily, verily, I say unto you, Whatsoever ye shall ask the Father in my name, he will give it you. [24]Hitherto have ye asked nothing in my name: ask, and ye shall receive, that your joy may be full. **John 16:23-24,**

[17]And these signs shall follow them that believe; In my name shall they cast out devils; they shall speak with new tongues; [18]They shall take up serpents; and if they drink any deadly thing, it shall not hurt them; they shall lay hands on the sick, and they shall recover. **Mark 16:17-18**

It is so beautiful to know that the Christian now has the legal right to use the name of Jesus. We can use this name to cast out devils, heal the sick and to deal with every force of darkness. There no power anywhere that can withstand this name. With the ability we have to use the name of Jesus, we have a legal approach to God and a legal ground to receive answers to our prayers. With the wonderful name of Jesus, we are explicitly more than conquerors.

www.ingramcontent.com/pod-product-compliance
Ingram Content Group UK Ltd.
Pitfield, Milton Keynes, MK11 3LW, UK
UKHW020232250726
13967UKWH00001B/318